ALL AROUND THE WORLD
LAOS

by Kristine Spanier, MLIS

T0014771

pogo

Ideas for Parents and Teachers

Pogo Books let children practice reading informational text while introducing them to nonfiction features such as headings, labels, sidebars, maps, and diagrams, as well as a table of contents, glossary, and index.

Carefully leveled text with a strong photo match offers early fluent readers the support they need to succeed.

Before Reading

- "Walk" through the book and point out the various nonfiction features. Ask the student what purpose each feature serves.
- Look at the glossary together. Read and discuss the words.

Read the Book

- Have the child read the book independently.
- Invite him or her to list questions that arise from reading.

After Reading

- Discuss the child's questions. Talk about how he or she might find answers to those questions.
- Prompt the child to think more. Ask: Agriculture is important in Laos. Do crops grow where you live? What are they?

Pogo Books are published by Jump!
5357 Penn Avenue South
Minneapolis, MN 55419
www.jumplibrary.com

Copyright © 2022 Jump!
International copyright reserved in all countries. No part of this book may be reproduced in any form without written permission from the publisher.

Library of Congress Cataloging-in-Publication Data

Names: Spanier, Kristine, author.
Title: Laos / by Kristine Spanier, MLIS.
Description: Minneapolis, MN: Jump!, Inc., [2022]
Series: All around the world | Audience: Ages 7-10
Identifiers: LCCN 2020055078 (print)
LCCN 2020055079 (ebook)
ISBN 9781636900117 (hardcover)
ISBN 9781636900124 (paperback)
ISBN 9781636900131 (ebook)
Subjects: LCSH: Laos—Juvenile literature.
Classification: LCC DS555.3 .S65 2022 (print)
LCC DS555.3 (ebook) | DDC 959.4—dc23
LC record available at https://lccn.loc.gov/2020055078
LC ebook record available at https://lccn.loc.gov/2020055079

Editor: Jenna Gleisner
Designer: Molly Ballanger

Photo Credits: Siam Muang Yim/Shutterstock, cover; stockphoto mania/Shutterstock, 1; Pixfiction/Shutterstock, 3; Korkiat Wijitchot/Shutterstock, 4; Sihi/Shutterstock, 5; Hvoenok/Shutterstock, 6-7; 06photo/Shutterstock, 7; jukurae/Shutterstock, 8-9tl; FLPA/SuperStock, 8-9tr; Norjipin Saidi/Shutterstock, 8-9bl; Agami Photo Agency/Dreamstime, 8-9br; Love Silhouette/Shutterstock, 10; hadynyah/iStock, 11; Education Images/Getty, 12-13; iStock, 14-15; bonchan/Shutterstock, 16; Ayotography/Shutterstock, 17; DEGAS Jean-Pierre/Hemis/SuperStock, 18-19; Surasak muangsuk/Shutterstock, 20-21; nednapa/Shutterstock, 23.

Printed in the United States of America at Corporate Graphics in North Mankato, Minnesota.

TABLE OF CONTENTS

CHAPTER 1

LANDLOCKED

Where can you view the Victory Gate? This **monument** is in Laos. It stands for freedom. It honors soldiers.

Victory Gate

Laos is in Southeast Asia. It is landlocked. This means it is surrounded by land. Mountains cover much of the country.

plumeria

The **climate** in Laos is **tropical**. The wet **monsoon** season is from May to October. Up to 90 inches (229 centimeters) of rain can fall. This means many plants grow.

The plumeria is the **national** flower. Palm and bamboo trees grow in forests.

bamboo ·····▶

Wild oxen and tigers live in the forests. Gibbons swing in the trees. Geckos and skinks crawl. The Mekong wagtail flies near the Mekong River.

DID YOU KNOW?

The elephant is the national animal of Laos. It stands for strength. Does your country have a national animal? What is it?

wild ox

gibbon

skink

Mekong wagtail

CHAPTER 2

LIFE IN LAOS

About half the people here are **Buddhist**. **Temples** are in most villages. The Great Stupa is the most important one in Laos. It is even shown on **currency** here.

Great Stupa

Many schools in Laos do not have enough books or materials. Most children finish at least five years of school. Some get more, but many children need to help at home.

rice plants

Most people here farm. Rice is the biggest **crop**. Sweet potatoes, corn, and sugarcane grow here, too.

Some farmers raise **livestock**. Water buffalo and cattle graze in fields.

WHAT DO YOU THINK?

Most families here work together on farms. How do you help your family? Would you like to farm? Why or why not?

People in Laos vote for members of the National Assembly. The assembly meets in Vientiane. This is the **capital**.

Assembly members vote for a president. This person is the head of state. The president then picks a prime minister. This person leads the government.

Vientiane

government building

CHAPTER 3

FOOD AND FUN

Thum mak hoong is a popular salad. It is made with shredded papaya. Sticky rice is served with most meals.

sticky rice

thum mak hoong

In October, people watch boat races on the Mekong River. Each boat can hold up to 50 people!

Baci **ceremonies** mark special occasions. People perform them at home. They gather around a pyramid of marigold flowers. They tie white strings around their wrists. They pray and wish for good luck.

TAKE A LOOK!

Baci ceremonies celebrate many events. Take a look!

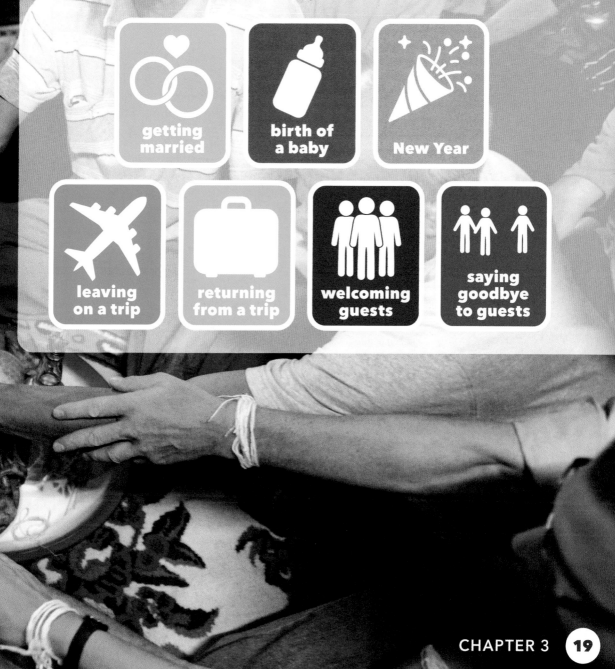

getting married

birth of a baby

New Year

leaving on a trip

returning from a trip

welcoming guests

saying goodbye to guests

The New Year in Laos is in April. People celebrate for three days. They watch parades and listen to music. They go to art shows and sports events.

There is so much to see in Laos! Would you like to visit?

WHAT DO YOU THINK?

Water **symbolizes** a fresh start. People in Laos splash it on one another. They wish each other a happy new year. How do you celebrate each new year?

QUICK FACTS & TOOLS

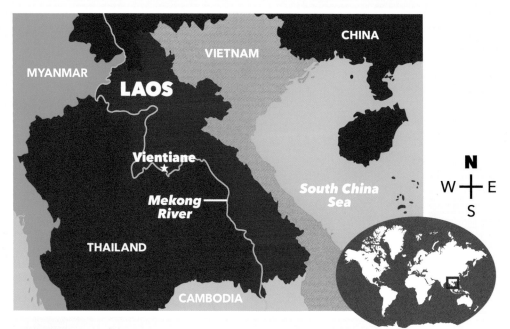

LAOS

Location: Southeast Asia

Size: 91,429 square miles (236,800 square kilometers)

Population: 7,447,396 (July 2020 estimate)

Capital: Vientiane

Type of Government: communist state

Languages: Lao, French, English

Exports: wood products, coffee, electricity, tin, copper, gold

Currency: Lao kip

GLOSSARY

Buddhist: People who follow and practice Buddhism. Buddhism is a religion or way of life that focuses on spiritual development.

capital: A city where government leaders meet.

ceremonies: Formal events that mark important occasions.

climate: The weather typical of a certain place over a long period of time.

crop: A plant grown for food.

currency: The form of money used in a country.

livestock: Animals that are kept or raised on a farm or ranch.

monsoon: A season or storm that brings heavy rain.

monument: A statue, building, or other structure that reminds people of an event, person, or group.

national: Of, having to do with, or shared by a whole nation.

symbolizes: Represents a concept or an idea.

temples: Buildings used for worship.

tropical: Of or having to do with the hot, rainy area of the tropics.

Lao currency

INDEX

TO LEARN MORE

Finding more information is as easy as 1, 2, 3.

❶ Go to www.factsurfer.com

❷ Enter "Laos" into the search box.

❸ Choose your book to see a list of websites.

FACT SURFER